AF413153

If you could leap high high high

reaching toward the wide blue sky

not as high as bird or plane

but high enough to freedom gain

barely touching paw to limb

then launching higher once again

If you could drop and twist and twirl

and quickly tail and legs unfurl

to land with ease on all four feet

and calmly walk on down the street

you would know and feel and see

how grand it is to be like me

AUNTIE
PAWSWORTH'S

FELINE ADVICE
COLUMN

Letting the domestic cat out of the bag
The good, the bad, and the ugly

C.S. NEAL & A.A. THEODOSIS

AUNTIE PAWSWORTH'S FELINE ADVICE COLUMN

Copyright © 2024 by C. S. Neal and A.A. Theodosis

Published by C Neal Designs Publishing
ISBN 979-8-218-10953-0

Typeset by The Book Refinery Ltd

Cover and internal illustrations by Slavica Zivanovic
Cover designed using images from Freepik.com
Cat in tree image courtesy of beakraus
Catatonka persona adopted with permission of A-Boy Neal
Yin-yang cat illustration courtesy of Pixabay.com

Requests for permissions should be addressed to:
C Neal Designs Publishing
Post Office Box 3343
Beverly Hills, CA 90212 USA

CONTENTS

CATS DAILY

Dear Readers,

Welcome to *Cats Daily*—a newspaper written by cats for cats and for people who are interested in cats. This book features a selection of inquiries submitted to our advice columnist, Philomena Pawsworth. A Bengal cat of mixed heritage who was adopted into a large human family, Philomena has spent over a decade studying human beings in a dynamic urban environment requiring novel adaptive behaviors. She mastered the myriad challenges confronting cats in modern America and has built a unique bridge of understanding between the often baffling worlds of the human and the cat. When asked about just a few of the qualities required to successfully navigate these two domains, Philomena suggests curious intelligence, extroversion, determination, mental and physical agility, persistence, a sense of playfulness, and getting a minimum of fifteen hours of sleep each day. Although Philomena credits distinguished Abyssinians in her maternal lineage for gifting her with these traits, she believes all of us can work on cultivating them to various degrees. We look forward to additional insights from Philomena in *Auntie Pawsworth's Feline Advice Column.*

The earliest known advice column appeared in the year 1690 in a London periodical, *The Athenian Mercury*, published twice weekly by The Athenian Society. It is reportedly the first periodical that catered specifically to women and the columns covered questions regarding the natural sciences, religion, literature, and politics.

In the United States advice columns began to appear in newspapers starting in the 1880s. They dealt primarily with domestic work, such as answering questions related to sewing and recipes. Contemporary life-advice columns mostly respond to questions on relationships and social interactions—the challenges of heart, home, and culture. *Dear Abby*, a popular syndicated column written by Abigail Van Buren, is a notable example. Although a plethora of online sites treat topics dealing with animals, including cats, *Auntie Pawsworth's Feline Advice Column* presents a rare opportunity for a cosmopolitan cat, continuing the tradition of columnists recorded in the journals and newspapers of yore, to lend her voice to some of the most pressing issues affecting cats and cat caretakers today.

We are also treated to the work of our resident philosopher, Catatonka ("Buffalo Cat"), who offers subsequent commentary—*Catatonka Says*—to each of the columns. A Native American Shorthair, Catatonka provides restrained counterpoint to *Auntie Pawsworth's* spirited replies.

The Editors

Catatonka Says

THE FAST AND THE FURIOUS

Dear Auntie Pawsworth,

I'm a Maine Coon cat with a large, fluffy tail. My tail is my sensitive sail. I walk with it proudly hoisted in the air as a welcoming gesture and symbol of my manly cathood. My lady gently strokes my head and shoulders, but her grandchildren are another story. When they visit, it's as if all the demons from Hades have been let loose in the household. They run around screeching and try to pull my tail. MEOUCH! It takes all my willpower to prevent myself from scratching their arms to the bone! How do I get these mouthy munchkins to understand that I like being petted but my tail is off limits?

Roman

Dear Roman,

I love your name. It is perfect for a big male Maine Coon. It reminds me of the centurions who commanded Roman legions. About the grandtwits—best not to scratch them. I applaud your willpower. The most obvious solution is to disappear when they arrive on scene. What they cannot see, they cannot touch. The instant they reach for you, turn your billowing sail into the wind and head for the Hebrides. No kid on the planet can outrun a cat. Many children are kind and gentle with animals, while others behave like Tasmanian Devils. Give them several more years to grow a brain. If you skedaddle when they start to grab your fluffy appendage, their attention will soon be diverted elsewhere and you can gleefully spy on them from a safe and secret place, turning the tails, as it were!

Auntie Pawsworth

Catatonka says

A RIDE ON THE WILD SIDE

Dear Auntie Pawsworth,

We've been invaded! Every week the closet door is opened and out comes a bizarre object, a disk that moves on its own throughout the house, whirling around as it collides with walls or the furniture. I've tried staring it down—doesn't work. I've growled at it, pounced at it, and slapped at it, but it ignores me. I don't want to get too close to it until I figure it out. What is this intimidating thing that is let loose in my home and what can I do about it?

Patti Cat

Dear Patti Cat,

Let's *Roomba!* You have not been invaded by an alien life form, although it may seem so. The menacing disk that is released from the dark depths of the closet is in fact a round robotic vacuum cleaner that is sweeping up untidy bits of dirt and hair from the floors of your home. One of the most popular brands is *Roomba.* Most cats are curious and love the challenge of exploring something new. You are missing a great opportunity. Instead of challenging the thing, jump on it and sit down for a thrilling ride. As you have observed, the machine will bump into an object, wheel around, and head across the floor until it bumps into another object. The bumping and twirling are great fun! Take advantage of the free rides. There are not that many in life. Trust me, I know!

Auntie Pawsworth

CATATONKA SAYS

ARISTOCAT

Dear Auntie Pawsworth,

You seem to understand how humans think. I don't. I'm a Toyger with a wonderful family, but they do one thing that annoys me. For some unholy reason they tie a bonnet on my head and coo over me while wheeling me around in a landau. It's humiliating. Are all cats forced to endure this kind of embarrassment?

Stéphane, from Paris, France

Dear Stéphane,

Bonjour to our friend across the large pond! No, not all humans treat their pets like babies, but many do. They enjoy dressing them up (a "toy tiger" would be quite a temptation) and are thrilled when people admire their little ones. *C'est la vie.* You might be uncomfortable in the restrictive clothing and you might not understand a word people are saying, but there is a silver lining inside that fluffy bonnet of yours—you no doubt receive a lot of attention. Since your family is determined to display you in public, learn to enjoy it. Consider your cap a royal crown. You are a furry Charlemagne. Transform that forlorn look into a confident smirk and wave a regal paw to all who pass!

Auntie Pawsworth

CATATONKA SAYS

A FAST GETAWAY

Dear Auntie Pawsworth,

What a thrill! In what my family calls "the bathroom" is the object of one of my favorite pastimes—a roll of paper that I unwind at rapid speed. It's exciting to watch the soft white tissue flow to the floor in a great heap. But, oh, the shouting that comes afterwards! My "Dad" doesn't seem to appreciate my play and chases me out of the bathroom with wild gestures. What is the issue with the tissue?

Yanni

Dear Yanni,

I bet you can slap that roll of tissue onto the floor faster than a Model S Plaid Tesla can accelerate—0 to 60 in under two seconds! Woohoo! The thing is, what we consider a fantastic source of fun means something entirely different to your family. To them the roll of paper is utilitarian, definitely something not to be unwound in a flash into a heap on the floor. My advice is to redirect your prodigious energy to other pastimes like catching field mice or chasing territorial intruders. But if you find you cannot resist the urge to paw the tissue into mounds of fibrous mashed potatoes, then you will just have to *roll* with the consequences! I suggest another burst of speed, making a mad dash past your Dad before he wraps you like a mummy in all that bathroom tissue!

Auntie Pawsworth

When confronted with an
unhappy energy force,
it is best to make a
hasty retreat.

LOVE OR LIST?

Dear Auntie Pawsworth,

I'd like to take advantage of your expertise on cats to ask your advice. My husband and our two boys aged ten and twelve are at odds with our sweet cat, Tiger. Lately, when we try to pet him, Tiger claws and bites in response. The vet said he is healthy, but Tiger's behaviors continue to be aggressive. My husband, who has been mildly bitten twice, is threatening to put Tiger up for adoption on Craig's List. What can I do?

Debbie, Tiger's Mom

Dear Debbie,

Love, not list. Clawing and controlled biting are kitty saying, "No, don't do that!" There are three males in the household—maybe they have been teasing Tiger? Give Tiger extra attention and warn household males large and small to treat Tiger with gentleness and respect. If the adversarial behavior continues, I recommend listing hubby and the boys on Craig's List for adoption to a new home. You and Tiger can then settle comfortably onto the sofa in front of the television with a good movie (suggestion: *Oliver & Company*) and a bowl of tasty treats.

Auntie Pawsworth

CATATONKA SAYS

DIM ITRI
SOCKS

WHAT'S IN A NAME?

Dear Auntie Pawsworth,

A friend is moving out of town to take care of her elderly parents, and I have agreed to adopt her lovely cat Dimitri. I am thrilled, as I love the cat. But I am not comfortable with his name, as nice as it is, and would tend to use unflattering diminutives like "Dimi" or worse "Dim." I prefer to name him with something more cat-like such as "Speckles" or "Socks." How long will it take for him to learn a new name? Will it confuse him?

New Kitty Mom, Alegria

Dear Alegria,

I just love these stories. You deserve a Feline Mom of the Year award for adopting Dimitri. About a new name: Most human speech sounds like oral scrambled eggs to kitty ears. The way to teach Dimitri his new name is to attach it to the end of his current name (Dimitri-**Speckles** or Dimitri-**Socks**), emphasizing the new portion of the name whenever you feed him, pet him, or give him treats. In a few shakes of a cat's tail, you can eliminate Dimitri and just use his new name. But do let us drop "Dim" or "Dimi." After all, some cats are smarter than a lot of human beings. Meow!

Auntie Pawsworth

Catatonka says

MEMPHIS BLUES

Dear Auntie Pawsworth,

I have spent decades cleaning up after cats. They have a hair ball—they vomit. They eat grass—they vomit. They wait too long to eat—they vomit. They eat too much—they vomit. They eat too fast—they vomit. A change in food—they vomit. I'm losing my mind over this and I am done with it all!

Mona in Memphis

Dear Mona,

And your point is? Yes, we felines were created with sensitive digestive tracts that react to issues related to food and fur. Regurgitating fur balls is no fun. Would you like to have a massive hair ball blocking your intestines? Think what it is like to have a single hair caught in your mouth. Disgusting! But since you have lived with cats for decades you surely know the rewards. Cats are marvelous companions. I take the liberty of noting that the cats in your household have lived with your irritations as well, which include various organic bodily disturbances and floating human hair and skin cells (yuck!) which you shed every two to four weeks. On behalf of felines everywhere, I suggest focusing on the fine qualities of our species. Disgorge any negative feelings you are entertaining, just as if they were an uncomfortable hair ball. You will feel better afterwards!

Auntie Pawsworth

CATATONKA SAYS

OF MAD DOGS AND MOSH PITS

Dear Auntie Pawsworth,

Help! Our family is blaming us for the racket made by our neighbor's dogs! We are two quiet cats, but our favorite window overlooks the neighbor's front yard, where three noisy terriers live. When anyone passes their yard, or when they see us sitting on the window sill, they bark excitedly, spin around, and smash into each other like mad dogs in a mosh pit. It's great fun to watch! Unfortunately we're scolded for the racket made by the terriers. It's not our fault that they yip and yap all day, yet we are forced to leave our window seat. Why should we be deprived of our entertainment?

Tammy and Toggles

Dear Tammy and Toggles,

I sympathize. However, as part of a loving family, you should contribute to its peace and well-being. You might try your outdoor viewing from other windows in your home and stay away from the one that overlooks your neighbor's neurotic dogs. It will help quiet their canine concerto, and your people will love you for it. They may even nominate you for twin Feline Nobel Peace Prizes. But, just between the three of us, as a cat I cannot resist—when the family is away, time to play! Plop down on that window seat and enjoy the show! Meow!

Auntie Pawsworth

CATATONKA SAYS

SIMPLY SIAMESE

Dear Auntie Pawsworth,

I am so thrilled to be able to communicate with you. Contrary to having a complaint, I want to express my appreciation for my lady, Marylou. She is an angel. She has provided a large, beautiful home which I never tire of exploring, and she treats me kindly. She is always attentive and caring. She also understands my nature and never complains about anything I do. I love the entire family, from the elders, to the feisty, energetic youngsters. Every day is a joy!

Leiza, a Siamese

Dear Leiza,

Thank you for writing this lovely expression of appreciation for your family. How refreshing it is to read that the household members understand your personality and particular needs. Siamese cats have many wonderful qualities. You and your cousins are sophisticated, love attention, are endlessly curious, and talkative. You may remember the dialogue from the Disney movie, *Lady and the Tramp*: "We are Siamese if you please. We are Siamese if you don't please." Your intelligence and demanding personality add to the royal mystique of your classical lineage. You are, indeed, the privileged princess of your domain!

Auntie Pawsworth

CATATONKA SAYS

Faithfulness and sincerity
are among the highest
virtues.

THE CAT BOX

Dear Auntie Pawsworth,

Oh my gosh! It seems like I'm continually in a jam. David, my guardian, loves golf. He practices in the living room, hitting his golf balls along the hallway and into the utility room where my litter box is located. I love batting those balls and chasing them across the floor, but every time I do David yells, "Stop it! Get outta here!" I don't like making him angry, but those little rolling white balls are irresistible! What do you recommend?

Jeffie Tom Cat

Dear Jeffie,

Seeing golf balls roll across the floor in all directions is a temptation for sure. I am getting a tingle just visualizing them. But there is nothing worse than a frustrated golfer. Each fancies himself to be Phil Mickelson or Tiger Woods and does not appreciate anything that interferes with his efforts. I suggest cultivating a little willpower. When David starts whacking away, do not chase the balls and bat them out of line. Instead, wait…wait for it… There it is! One of those balls has landed in the sand trap. That's your domain. It is your turn now. Throw some litter over that ball. *Finders, keepers!* When David gives up his game, you are free to take your bunker shot and hit that ball out of the sand. All is fair in love and golf. *"Fore!"*

Auntie Pawsworth

An urgent desire to have
things prevents best
outcomes.
Patience rewards.

IT HERTZ!

Dear Auntie Pawsworth,

I am an indoor cat, yet my ears are burning from loud, incessant sounds. Why must humans be so noisy? They play music, slam doors, run the vacuum, the garbage disposal, the automatic can opener, the dishwasher, the car, mixers and mowers and motorcycles. It's maddening! Often I hide in a closet to get away from the constant racket. Do they really need to make this much noise?

Rob the Ragamuffin

Dear Rob,

I am so sorry. Ragamuffins are affectionate, friendly, gentle, and calm. How upsetting it must be, all the stress on those poor ears. Unrelenting noise is normal for humans and, alas, a part of modern life. The juggernaut of sound can cause aural whiplash, like dangling on the side of a speeding train, one's body being whipped by the wind and exposed to the fierce whoosh of the wheels and the nervous clacking of the tracks. It makes one's fur stand on end. The thing is, cats have superior hearing. Our ears can detect sound at an ultrasonic level, frequencies higher than the upper audible limit of human hearing. Sound is measured by vibrations per second called *frequency* with a unit of measurement called *hertz*. We can hear one hundred thousand hertz. Compare dogs, whose range is thirty-five thousand to forty thousand hertz. And humans? Their hearing only measures a measly twenty thousand hertz. Since an outside escape does not seem an option (not that it would be any less irritating), a closet is perhaps the best solution. If it is a linen closet, nestle into the fresh, fluffy towels. May you dream peacefully, lulled by muffled sounds, and awaken feeling relaxed and ready to take on the world again, knowing you have a quiet refuge whenever sound overwhelms. Happy Zzzzs.

Auntie Pawsworth

CATATONKA SAYS

BEVERLY HILLS LITTER

Dear Auntie Pawsworth,

I've always lived with cats. I love them, but the one thing I still can't stand is litter being tracked all over the house. Having to sweep and vacuum daily to keep from stepping on gravelly bits everywhere I walk is really tedious. Can you suggest an effective remedy?

Berenda in Beverly Hills

Dear Berenda,

Untidy cats in Beverly Hills? How about a magical broom like the one in Disney's *Fantasia* or a more modern version like a *Roomba* to do the sweeping for you? I also recommend that you purchase a textured mat or two to place at the base of the litter box to catch most of the litter as the kitties leap out of the box. Home goods stores have some very nice ones that retain the litter in a grid, allowing you to then dump the litter back into the box. But I think you should have some compassion for the cats in your life, based on domestic irritations inflicted upon them. They are forced to use litter boxes and try to be discreet, burying the litter to the best of their ability. As they push through the grit it becomes caught in their paws and is extremely uncomfortable. How would you like to walk around with gravel trapped between your toes? I would not wish it on my worst enemy. Well, maybe…

Auntie Pawsworth

CATATONKA SAYS

A FLUTTER OF LOVE

Dear Auntie Pawsworth,

My cat Sipsy has been with me for fifteen years through thick and thin. She is a tender, affectionate little animal and very amusing. She also greets me at the door every day when I arrive home from work. I jingle my keys as I approach the door so that she knows it is me, then I call her name before I enter. On the other side of the door I always hear a soft mew in response. I just love hearing that sweet little greeting. The reason I'm writing is that Sipsy engages in a behavior that I don't understand, even after all these years. She sits, staring at me, and slowly lowers and raises her eyelids. Really slowly. It's not a normal blink. What is she doing?

Sandy

Dear Sandy,

You noted that Sipsy is tender and affectionate. She is demonstrating her affection for you with this specific form of blinking. When she lazily closes and reopens her eyes, it is the ultimate compliment. She is showing that she is comfortable and happy with you. People are key social partners for domestic animals who often spend more time with human family members than with others of their own species. It is wonderful when we understand each other. Sipsy is smiling at you. Blink slowly back at her. You are bonding!

Auntie Pawsworth

Catatonka Says

WAFFLING

Dear Auntie Pawsworth,

My cat is named Waffle. Waffle is a real boy. He loves roughhousing. And I love playing with him. But, you know cats. Waffle plops down on his side, gripping my hands with his front claws and ripping away with his rear ones. He's strong. By the time we finish our play session, my hands are shredded. I have to wash them and treat them with antibiotic ointment. Waffle gets the exercise he needs and is always happy after our skirmishes, and that makes me happy, but I suffer the consequences. How can I avoid injury while playing with Waffle?

Abraham

Dear Abraham,

If only all human dads were like you! I commend you for loving Waffle and for your willingness to provide the stimulation he needs for his physical and mental well-being. Some cats are tender of disposition and do not like rough treatment. Others, like Waffle—oh boy! They are the feline Conor McGregor or Dustin Poirier. They enjoy a good grapple which, in the cat world, includes the use of teeth and claws. Since you do not have a thick layer of fur, you need some PPE, personal protective equipment. In your kitchen you may have a common item, an oven mitt. It is padded with a place for your thumb and fingers and will allow Waffle to rip loose during your play-fighting sessions. Just one tiny admonition: Since you will be wearing a defensive mitt, the temptation might be to be play more aggressively than usual with Waffle, overpowering and frustrating him. Go a bit easy. His little feline ego will be happier if you "cry uncle" and allow Waffle the ultimate win. Meow!

Auntie Pawsworth

CATATONKA SAYS

BOBO THE EAR BENDER

Dear Auntie Pawsworth,

BoBo, my eleven-year-old tabby, talks to me constantly. It is really frustrating because I would love to be able to understand what he is saying. I can figure out most of what he wants, but sometimes I'm not sure. I also notice that he and my other cat do not meow at each other unless they are in a serious skirmish and the other cat yowls. That's the only time I hear verbal communication between the two of them, so I have to believe that the meowing is intended for me. Am I right?

Penelope from Perth

Dear Penelope,

G'day mate! Yes, BoBo is talking to you, but do not assume that he is just being chatty. It is a request of some kind. He might want you to pet him, he might want to play, he might want to go outside, he might be hungry, maybe the litter box needs cleaning, he might be letting you know he is getting ready to disgorge a fur ball; but he is definitely talking to you. As with all intelligent living creatures, BoBo's imperative is to find a way to get his daily physical and emotional needs met. That means communicating with you. Your determination to understand what BoBo is telling you will be rewarded. It is exciting when the aha! light bulbs turn on: *"I didn't know that's what you want! Now I get it!"*

Auntie Pawsworth

A thing seems impossible
until you discover it isn't.

A SNIFF IN KIND

Dear Auntie Pawsworth,

Sometimes my cat Fluffer does a goofy thing. Whenever I'm reading or just relaxing while lying on the bed or sofa, she jumps up and sniffs my face, especially around the area of my mouth. I don't mind it. It just seems kind of odd. Afterwards she snuggles next to me for a cat nap. Why is she sniffing my face?

Sara in Sedona

Dear Sara,

It is an expression of love. When Fluffer sniffs your face, it is one of the ways she is recognizing you as someone she cares for. A cat's sense of smell is the primary way it identifies people and objects. Cats have more than two hundred million odor sensors in their noses in comparison to humans, who have just five million. We love to smell everything, from each and every shopping bag you bring home filled with exotic scents to a stack of warm, fragrant, freshly dried laundry. Oooooh, the pleasure of it! Sniffing your face is a bonding moment between you and Fluffer. Go on, give her a good sniff back!

Auntie Pawsworth

Catatonka Says

HAIR CURRENTS

Dear Auntie Pawsworth,

I share my home with Thomas Tinkleton Touchington, a muscular mix who enjoys being petted. While I'm stroking him, I become fixated on his whiskers. I just love them. The ones above his eyes are black and protrude in every direction, so adorable! And the ones on either side of his mouth are long and white, reminding me of a walrus. I'm curious about what purpose whiskers actually serve.

Lorraine

Dear Lorraine,

This is an interesting topic. Whiskers are extensions of Thomas's skin and are designed to detect even the smallest changes in his environment such as air currents, air pressure, temperature, and wind direction. They detect the slightest contact and send signals to sensory cells at their roots. Cats' whiskers have not been studied like that of other animals such as walruses and seals, whose whiskers are most commonly used to locate food. For example, seals extend their whiskers to detect and follow the trails left in the water by fish. The natural world is thrilling. High time someone dives more deeply into the study of wonderful kitty whiskers.

Auntie Pawsworth

CATATONKA SAYS

MAKING BISCUITS

Dear Auntie Pawsworth,

Our kitty, Ellie, engages in a very sweet activity. She pushes her paws into soft things like the comforters on our beds, the throw rug in the entryway, and even our clothing when she sits on our laps. She becomes totally absorbed and is in a sort of trance. Is this a meditation thing for cats?

Connie from San Juan Capistrano

Dear Connie,

Oh, the joy of "making biscuits!" That's what the behavior is often called. Kneading soft things is pleasurable. It may come from the time when we were kittens and massaged our mothers' tummies as we fed, or there may be other reasons. It is one of the mysteries of life. Usually cats will knead before lying down for a nap, and you may hear Ellie meowing or purring while pumping those little paws. Hopefully you get as much pleasure watching Ellie as she derives from gently massaging soft things, including your sweaters. San Juan Capistrano—beautiful sunsets! Did the swallows return this year?

Auntie Pawsworth

CATATONKA SAYS

R.I.P.

Dear Auntie Pawsworth,

I need some advice, please. My large black Siberian cat, Angus, is continually returning to the house from an outdoor adventure and depositing dead critters on my kitchen floor. Sadly I have had to perform impromptu funeral services for an exquisite little hummingbird, its tiny feathers scattered about; mice; crickets; and bits of a gopher (yuck!). I'm not sure why Angus brings these victims to me. He doesn't eat them. I feel sorry for the little things each time I discover the result of Angus's latest exploit. How can I stop him?

Lynn in Los Angeles

Dear Lynn,

No, no, no. You cannot. Angus is acting upon a natural imperative. It is the stimulation of the chase and the conquering of prey. I begin to salivate, just thinking about it. Cats are genetically programmed to chase flitting or running creatures. And we like to share our prey with those with whom we live. Angus is bringing you gifts. Often it is to show appreciation for the affection we are given, to share a meal, or to seek approval for our catch. Angus will be Angus. The only way you can prevent him from bringing you the occasional gift is to transition him to living indoors. He will feel deprived of the pleasure of outdoor pursuits but will eventually adapt. Meanwhile, after you have disposed of the next *gift* and regained your composure, give Angus a hug. He will look up at you glowingly with his jewel-like eyes, reassured that Mom loves him and appreciates his hunting prowess.

Auntie Pawsworth

CATATONKA SAYS

A BUM RAP

Dear Auntie Pawsworth,

My name is Odie-Will and I live with my human mother. I love my Mom. She is kind and loving, plays with me, feeds me delicious food, and is the best Mom any cat could have. There's just one thing I don't understand about her. I don't know why she doesn't like it when I lift my tail and back up to her face. Every time I do it, she roughly pushes me aside. Why is she is rejecting me?

Odie-Will

Dear Odie-Will,

Your Mom is not rejecting you. She just does not understand kitty etiquette. Of course a proper greeting necessitates a good bum sniff! To Mom: Odie-Will is showing affection and is bonding with you when he offers you a good sniff of his nether region. It might seem odd to you, but this is how we acknowledge one another and it is natural for Odie-Will to extend this greeting to you. If you find a close-up of his bum objectionable, just gently turn him aside and stroke him affectionately. Over time you may even begin to enjoy Odie-Will's ritual greeting. On the other hand…

Auntie Pawsworth

Catatonka Says

THE JOY OF GIVING

Dear Auntie Pawsworth,

My interior household net worth is constantly being diminished. Things keep disappearing. I replace them, and they vanish again. It is really frustrating. I never saw anyone taking the objects and was totally mystified until one day… I walked into our mud room just in time to see the tip of a blanket being pulled around the edge of my back door. Quietly I peered out the door to see who the thief might be. It was my cat Solomon. There he was, dragging the blanket down the sidewalk to the doorstep of a neighbor. I have now discovered that Solomon gives gifts to all the neighbors. It really is astonishing. He steals everything—my towels, coats, caps, socks, shoes, throw cushions, figurines, even plastic utensils. What can I do about this behavior?

Anne from Tulsa

Dear Anne,

That Solomon takes gifts to the neighbors indicates he likes their reactions to his generosity. They may be responding with affection or food. Stopping Solomon's behavior may not be possible as long as your neighbors continue to interact with him. You might chat with them, suggesting that they not encourage Solomon, but for animal lovers the urge to engage is at times irresistible. Although you may be experiencing irritation as a consequence of his actions, Solomon is experiencing the truth of the axiom that there is more joy in giving than receiving. It is just that it is mostly your things that Solomon is giving away. Meow!

Auntie Pawsworth

CATATONKA SAYS

Trying to change the
habits of others is futile.
It is easier to change
one's self.

TOM FOOLERY

Dear Auntie Pawsworth,

My very favorite thing to do is play with rubber bands. I love to toss them into the air and try to catch them as they come back down. Sometimes, though, one of them will land on my head. I cry for my Mom until she comes to remove it for me. She thinks I'm silly for asking her for help and she teases me about it. But, as a cat, I know you understand and will be on my side.

Frank in Fort Worth

Dear Frank,

Sorry, I agree with your Mom. What a silly thing you are, not for tossing rubber bands but for whining when they land on your head. What a kitwit! Did it not occur to you to shake off the rubber band, remove it with your paw, or roll over on the floor until it comes off? Wailing is a cry for attention. While you are amusing yourself, your Mom may be busy with a hundred things humans do. She cannot always interrupt her activities to respond to you and may start tuning out your calls for help. In turn you might suffer as a result, like the bored shepherd boy in Aesop's fable *The Boy Who Cried Wolf.* Your proverbial nine lives are going to be seriously tested in the future. Now is the time to flip the switch to maturity and solve your own challenges. Meow!

Auntie Pawsworth

Excessive craving of
attention turns cat or
man into mush.

WHO'S THE BOSS?

Dear Auntie Pawsworth,

I have a dilemma. I work from home, or at least I try to. I have two male cats, Cool Hand Luke (Lukie) and Maverick. Whenever I want to pull up a chair to work at my desk, I find it occupied by one of the cats. Now I have been relegated to a small, hard-seated, metal patio chair, while the cats relax in comfort. I keep trying to convey to them that I am the alpha energy and they should defer to me, but neither seems impressed. Do you have a solution to offer?

Crazed Christina

Dear Crazed Christina,

Hahaha! We know who the alphas are in the household and who is the pretender to the throne. The cats have you wrapped around their little furry paws. Wherever you are, there they will be. Cats like being in the same room with their human family members and they always know the best seats in the house. Laugh at them, love them, and appreciate the amount of resistance and persistence that comes in small packages. You may as well give in. Between you and the cats—no contest!

Auntie Pawsworth

CATATONKA SAYS

PLEASE UNLEASH ME!

Dear Auntie Pawsworth,

I am an indoor cat, except when taken out of the house on a leash. To let my family know that I want to go out, I sit in front of the sliding glass door until they realize my intent. Then they put a leash on me and take me outside. I don't want to be constricted. I want to freely roam the back yard. Frustrated by this restriction, I just sit looking through the sliding glass door and eventually they take me back into the house. I think they believe I am just stupidly staring at my reflection in the glass. The whole routine is so odd. How can I get them to understand I want to go out without the leash?

Testy Tony

Dear Testy Tony,

What a dilemma. This fruitless activity would make anyone testy. I suggest noise. Stand at the door and vocalize until they respond. If they reach for the leash, dance around so that they cannot attach it to you. If they put the leash away and return to some other activity, go back to the door and meow again until they respond. Try wailing loudly, one meow tone over and over. It drives humans crazy. It is as annoying as someone relentlessly blowing a kazoo. Repetition usually wears down human resistance. Meow!

Auntie Pawsworth

CATATONKA SAYS

ON THE EDGE

Dear Auntie Pawsworth,

Swish! Boom! Bang! Thud! Crash! Ooooh, the pleasure of slowly pushing objects to the edge of the counter or table. Then that final, gentle shove. Wheeeee! Over it goes! What fun to hear the sounds and watch the object as it breaks into pieces or bounces and rolls across the floor. Is there anything better? But sometimes, just as I am about to give one last gentle push over the edge, someone in the family calls my name. I look up to see who it is, then I look back at that teetering object and give it the last little shove. Are my family members as thrilled as I am when I push things off the counter or table?

Lucky Cat

Dear Lucky Cat,

No, your family members are not thrilled. They are horrified by this behavior. They do not like to hear or see things break. We are playing with things they value. I know the temptation is hard to resist and that it is fun to push things toward the thrilling payoff of swish, boom, bang, thud and crash, but to avoid panicky screams you might wait until a time when members of the household are out for a few hours. Eventually though your guardians will return and you will face the consequences. You may have been lucky so far, but count how many of your fabled nine lives you have left because one day, with the brisk whisk of a broom, you might be swept out of the house to the sound of your own swish, boom, bang, thud and crash!

Auntie Pawsworth

CATATONKA SAYS

READING THE SIGNS

Dear Auntie Pawsworth,

My human family members don't get it. They don't seem to understand what I try to communicate to them. For instance, when I am unhappy or upset, I slam my tail from side to side. This statement is clear to every feline I know.

Why doesn't my family know what I am saying? Many times when I "speak" to them, they just look at me with a vacant stare. How long does it take for our families to "read the signs?"

Johnny Cat from Topanga Canyon

Dear Johnny Cat,

Maybe years. I know it is frustrating. Despite all that brainpower, humans are a little dense. If they had a tail to wag, maybe they would understand, but they generally have a difficult time reading body language. Cats are sensitive creatures and do not like being "rubbed the wrong way." We especially do not like being forced to do something we do not want to do. When we are agitated, the tail tells all. Be patient with your family. Some people are just "out there," like dangling participles, but let us hope that they will come to understand and appropriately respond to your signals. By the way, I love the beautiful California peaks and canyons, where our majestic mountain lion cousins still roam freely. Cheers!

Auntie Pawsworth

CATATONKA SAYS

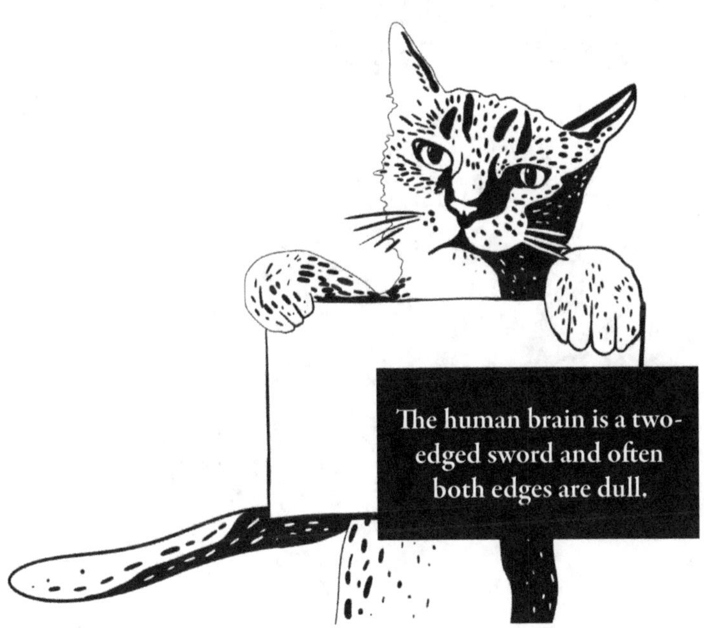

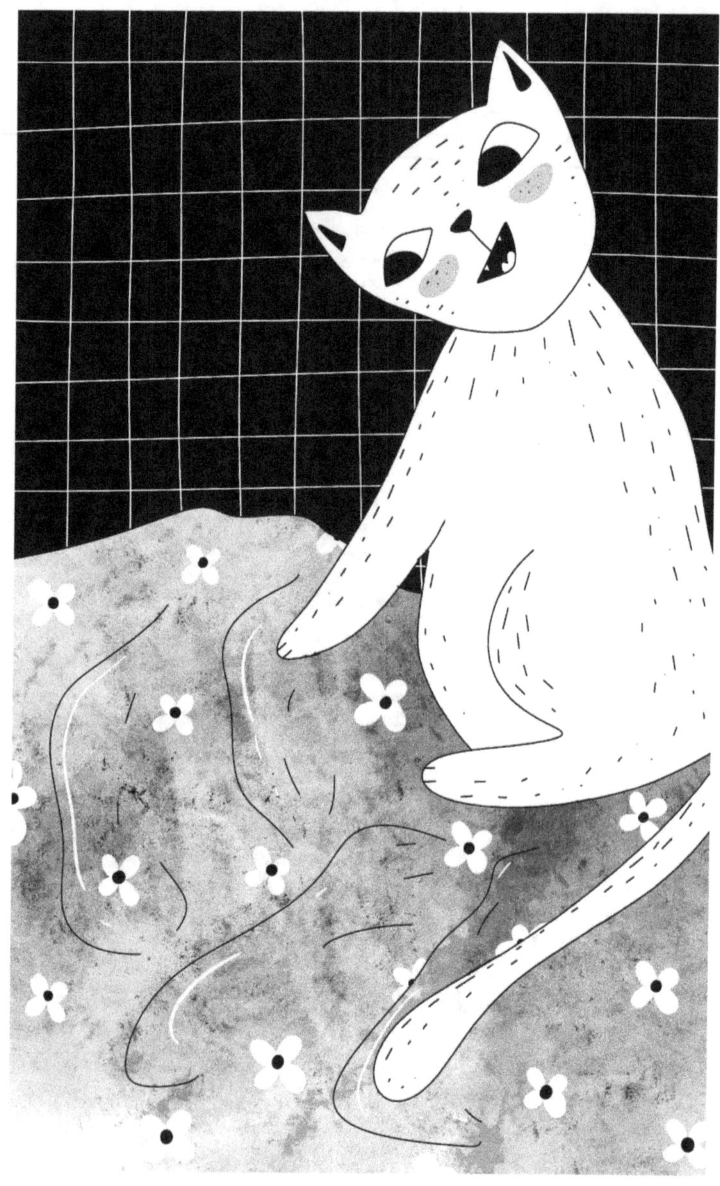

FOOT FETISH

Dear Auntie Pawsworth,

I notice that most of the cats and people who write to you present an issue of some kind for you to try to resolve. Not me. I want to share about the thrill I get from playing with human feet. When my Mom and Dad go to bed, they move their feet around under the covers and I can't resist attacking them. As I bite and thrash them with my paws, Mom is a little sensitive and tries to get out of the line of fire. My Dad laughs and thrashes back. When the fun winds down, I curl up for a good night's rest. I love my family!

Paisley, a Pixie-bob

Dear Paisley,

People may not understand this behavior, but I am with you on the attack of the bundled feet. I too like getting a good grip and thrashing away. I think it's probably as much fun as a dog thrusting its head out of a car window with its tongue lolling and the wind blowing against its face. Sheer joy! And what about the smell of sweaty feet and dirty socks? Meow! Better than the scent of Chanel No. 5! Love your letter. Thank you for sharing your passion for family and feet.

Auntie Pawsworth

CATATONKA SAYS

WHIFFERY

Dear Auntie Pawsworth,

I usually offer food straight out of the can, whether off the shelf or out of the refrigerator, to my cat Serendipity. Often Serendipity doesn't seem interested. He might sniff it and then leave it, coming back later to eat a bit more. He seems healthy, so I'm not sure why he is so finicky. Do you have any ideas?

Theresa in Tempe

Dear Theresa,

I hope you and Serendipity are staying cool in Arizona's sweltering heat. Taking a bite out of a familiar kitty playbook, Serendipity may just enjoy grazing, eating a portion of his food at meal time and saving some for later. On the other hand, the food may not be sufficiently aromatic. A cat's sense of taste is weak. Humans have thousands of taste buds but cats have under five hundred. They make up for this lack with a superior sense of smell, so their most powerful response to food is through scent, not taste. More aroma is released as the food warms to room temperature. To make the meal savory for Serendipity, you might try warming it a few seconds in your microwave or let the can sit in hot water for a time. The wafting smell of the food will likely have him chowing down with gusto. To Serendipity: *Bon appétit!*

Auntie Pawsworth

CATATONKA SAYS

GATLING GUNS

Dear Auntie Pawsworth,

We have just moved into a new home. I was worried about how long it might take for my cats to adjust to the change but, thankfully, they seem to have quickly acclimated themselves. My living room windows provide a wonderful view to a park with trees and flowers and a constant flow of beautiful butterflies and birds, and lovely scenes of people bicycling and walking their dogs. Blossom, my sweet Russian Blue, loves to watch the parade of activity. At times she gets excited and utters a sort of rapid staccato sound, a-a-a-a-a-a-a-a-a, as if she were firing a Gatling gun. What is the meaning of this weird chattering?

Margaret

Dear Margaret,

Cats are born hunters and share many traits with their cousins in the wild. Because Blossom is confined while observing animals outside, she may be expressing both excitement at seeing potential prey and frustration at not being able to stalk and pounce on the unwary insect, bird, or other small animal. You would be frustrated too if you were laser-focused on a highly desirable object that you were unable to attain. You might salivate or sigh. We fire Gatling guns! A-a-a-a-a-a-a-a!

Auntie Pawsworth

To reach the thing beyond
reach is the heart's desire
and the cause of much
anxiety.

SWEET DREAMS

Dear Auntie Pawsworth,

When I go to bed at night my kitty, Marianna, likes to fall asleep on my chest. It's sweet, but I can't read my book or do anything else until she finally moves aside. She seems so content. I don't like to disturb her. The question is, why does she insist on this routine every evening? Do all domestic cats do this?

Sam

Dear Sam,

No, not all cats like to rest on a person's chest, but many do. Your warmth and the sound of your heartbeat are soothing, helping to lull Marianna to sleep. *What do they dream of, these cats of mine, after keeping me awake and demanding my time? Are they slurping saucers of rich frothy cream, or tossing stuffed mice until they split at the seams?*

It is a compliment to you that Marianna feels comfortable enough to fall asleep on your chest, and I commend you for your patience and love for Marianna, allowing her to do so. Many human beings ignore the needs of their domestic animals. Clearly Marianna is a lucky kitty. May you both have sweet dreams.

Auntie Pawsworth

Catatonka Says

CATS DAILY

TENDER MERCIES

Dear Auntie Pawsworth,

Cats are so different from dogs. Our Golden Retriever, Lance, loves visitors and greets each one at the door with a welcoming bark and friendly tail wagging. Catilda ("Catty"), our rescued kitty, is the opposite. She hides whenever visitors arrive, even when they are members of our own family. Catty is such a sweet, loving little animal. We feel sorry that she is fearful. Will she always hide from visitors, do you think, or will she adapt at some point?

Sherry and Melinda

Dear Sherry and Melinda,

Some cats are friendly to family and strangers alike. Others prefer to assess people and situations before presenting themselves. What were Catty's earlier life experiences? It may be that someone treated her harshly and she is therefore particularly cautious, remembering suffering she may have endured. That she is well-loved and tenderly treated by you and your immediate family and that she has a safe, secure home is the most important thing. In time Catty may venture out to meet visitors, or she may prefer to always stay hidden, observing the activity from a safe space. Either way, it is best to let Catty make those decisions and for you and your family members to continue to respect her needs. Thank you for loving your rescued kitty. So many more need to be adopted by warm, caring families.

Auntie Pawsworth

Catatonka Says

SNUGGLE BUDDIES

Dear Auntie Pawsworth,

My human Mom and Dad love to cuddle in the evening on our sofa as they watch their favorite programs on television. I snuggle down between them. The advantage is that when one isn't petting me, the other one is. And if they seem to forget I'm there, it only takes a quiet mew to get their attention again. I adore being stroked. Ripples run through my whole body. It is a wonderful feeling, almost electrical, isn't it?

Mary, an American Shorthair

Dear Mary,

You are a placid breed of cat that gets along with all of the people in your life. You will provide your family with many years of loving companionship and clearly you have a family that is deserving of your affection. It seems you have cleverly found the perfect cuddle arrangement for maximum attention. An electrical thrill? Yes! Each hair has many nerve endings which evoke responses from our nervous system. Our heart rate slows, our muscles loosen, and our body relaxes. Many cats who were not exposed to human contact as kittens resist being petted or being held. Sadly, they do not know what they are missing. Man, woman, child, animal—all need the positive mental and physical benefits that accrue from a soft touch, the primary language of compassion. I envy your perfect cuddle arrangement. I love being petted. Stroke me! Meow!

Auntie Pawsworth

CATATONKA SAYS

AFTERWORD

Dear Readers,

Our introductory journey through *Auntie Pawsworth's Feline Advice Column* has come to a conclusion. We appreciate the cats and caregivers who wrote for advice and thank Philomena Pawsworth and Catatonka, our feline philosopher, for their candid responses. We hope you were amused and sometimes enlightened by the columns and encourage you to share through letters to the publisher your unique experiences, questions, and comments related to the wonderful world of cats. Meow for now!

The Editors

Our memories are filled with the impressions of those we have loved and among the most treasured are those of our kitties.

SUBJECTS TOUCHED UPON BY
AUNTIE PAWSWORTH'S FELINE ADVICE COLUMN

According to the Cat Fanciers Association, although the Abyssinian is one of the oldest known breeds, its origin remains inconclusive. The source of the name is not because Abyssinia, the former name of Ethiopia, was thought to be the confirmed birthplace of these cats, but because the first cats called "Abyssinians" that were exhibited in shows in England were said to have been imported from that general region. The first of this breed to be brought to North America from England arrived in the early 1900s, but it was not until the late 1930s that several high quality Abyssinians were exported from Britain to found today's American breeding programs.

It has been noted that this breed wasn't listed on their manifests, but these cats were likely among the passengers and crew that disembarked from the first ships that arrived at Plymouth, Massachusetts in 1620 and may have made their way to the New World even earlier on ships that carried settlers to the Jamestown colony in Virginia, Spanish explorers to Florida, and Vikings to Newfoundland. As excellent rat-catchers, they were valuable

The Maine Coon is a native New Englander, originating in the state of Maine, where they were popular mousers, farm cats and, likely ships' cats, at least as far back as the early nineteenth century. Maine Coons are big cats. The record for the world's longest house cat belongs to a Maine Coon who grew to be over four feet long.

A relatively recent domestic breed that originated in the northwestern United States, the Pixie-bob was intentionally bred to resemble the red bobcats found in the mountains of the Pacific Northwest. It has a stocky athletic build, large bone structure, and long, heavy legs. Its hind legs are a bit longer than the front ones, giving the Pixie-bob a rolling gait similar to that of true wild felines. Friendly, outgoing cats with an almost dog-like devotion to their human family members, they crave companionship, affection, and attention. The Pixie-bob is intelligent, respectful, and playful.

The Ragamuffin is a nice combination of sweet and smart, often described as puppy-like for its friendly personality and willingness to play fetch, learn tricks, and walk on a leash. Ragamuffins greet visitors warmly and are known for their docile nature.

The Toyger (Toy Tiger) is a mixed breed cat, a cross between the Bengal and Domestic Shorthair tabbies. Affectionate, energetic and playful, these cats are also loving and cuddly, making excellent family cats.

Meow.

ABOUT THE AUTHORS

C. S. Neal is a former freelance journalist, magazine editor (*Hot Rod Industry News, PowerBoat Magazine*), television writer (*Dumbo's Circus*, an independent production for the Disney Channel), and private detective. That is where author and cat cross paths—one meddling investigator prompts the other.

A.A. Theodosis is experienced in the performing arts of classical dance and music, a world traveler, and a prodigious reader who particularly enjoys historical cat narratives.

Both authors currently reside in Los Angeles.